SandCastle™ Primeros Sonidos

# Yolanda y Yago

**Cathy Camarena, M.Ed., and Gloria B. Ruff, M.Ed.**

**Consulting Editors**
Lourdes Flores-Hanson, M.S.E., and Gloria Rosso-White

ABDO Publishing Company

capstone
www.capstoneclassroom.com

Credits
Curriculum Coordinator: Nancy Tuminelly
Cover and Interior Design and Production: Mighty Media
Child Photography: Steven Wewerka, Wewerka Photography
Photo Credits: AbleStock, Kelly Doudna, Tracy Kompelien, Photodisc, ShutterStock

ISBN 978-1-4966-0381-4 (paperback)

Printed in the United States of America in North Mankato, Minnesota.
072017 010653R

SandCastle™ books are created by a professional team of educators, reading specialists, and content developers around five essential components that include phonemic awareness, phonics, vocabulary, text comprehension, and fluency. All books are written, reviewed, and leveled for guided and early intervention reading, and designed for use in shared, guided, and independent reading and writing activities to support a balanced approach to literacy instruction.

**SandCastle Level: Beginning**

# Yy

ABCChDEFGH
IJKLLLMNÑOP
QRSTUVWXYZ

abcchdefgh
ijklllmnñop
qrstuvwxyz

Yolanda

Yago

yema

yoyo

yuca

yogur

yunque

Mira la .

El  es rojo.

Mira la .

El  es comida.

El  es pesado.

A Yolanda le gusta la yuca.

La yuca es verde.

Yago juega con su yoyo.

El yoyo es un juguete.

El yoyo es rojo.

El yoyo está en la yuca.

# ¿Cuáles de estas cosas comienzan con y?

# Más palabras que comienzan con y

yac

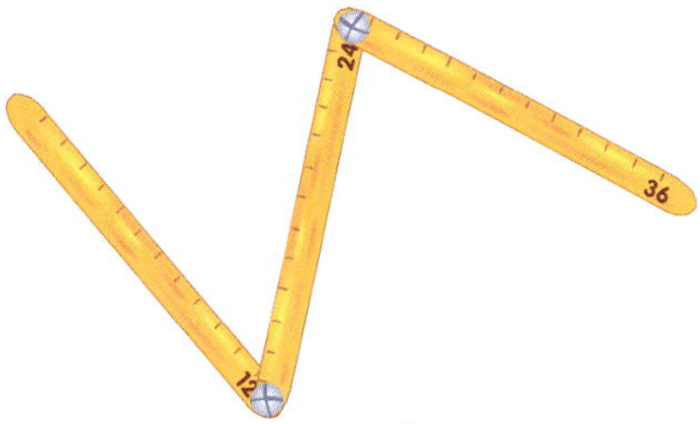


yarda

yate

yegua

yugo

# About SandCastle™

A professional team of educators, reading specialists, and content developers created the SandCastle™ series to support young readers as they develop reading skills and strategies and increase their general knowledge. The SandCastle™ series has four levels that correspond to early literacy development in young children. The levels are provided to help teachers and parents select the appropriate books for young readers.

**Emerging Readers**
(no flags)

**Beginning Readers**
(1 flag)

**Transitional Readers**
(2 flags)

**Fluent Readers**
(3 flags)

These levels are meant only as a guide. All levels are subject to change.

ABDO Publishing Company

**www.abdopub.com**

capstone

**www.capstoneclassroom.com**